Healthcare for All

People Over Profits

Dan Paul

ProAct 2525

Chapter 1

The Price of Waste in Healthcare

Healthcare in the United States is a paradox: it is both the most expensive system in the world and one riddled with inefficiencies and waste. This chapter examines the systemic issues that lead to wasted money, resources, and labor, preventing the realization of universal and effective healthcare for all. From excessive administrative costs to improper medication management, these inefficiencies reveal a system designed to prioritize profits over patient care.

The Cost of Administrative Waste

Administrative complexity is one of the most significant contributors to waste in the U.S. healthcare system. Unlike single-payer systems where billing processes are streamlined, the American system is characterized by:

- **Complex Billing and Coding**: Hospitals and providers must navigate a labyrinth of billing codes and processes, each varying by insurance company.

- **High Overhead Costs**: The need for prior authorizations, extensive paperwork, and claims processing inflates administrative overhead.

- **Duplication of Efforts**: Different systems and lack of standardization lead to redundant data entry and inefficiencies.

This administrative bloat diverts resources away from direct patient care, inflating costs while creating barriers for patients and providers alike.

Clinical Waste: Low-Value Care and Overprescription

Clinical waste arises from unnecessary or inappropriate medical practices, such as:

- **Unnecessary Tests and Procedures**: These often result from poor communication between providers or defensive medicine practices.

- **Overprescribing Medications**: Patients frequently receive medications they do not need, leading to financial waste and potential harm.

- **Ineffective Treatments**: Some treatments fail to consider the unique needs of patient populations, resulting in suboptimal outcomes.

- **Missed Preventative Care**: Opportunities to prevent illness are frequently overlooked, leading to more costly treatments down the line.

Operational Inefficiencies

Operational waste stems from poor management of healthcare resources, including:

- **Inefficient Scheduling**: Long patient wait times and provider idle time result from mismanaged appointment systems.
- **Underutilized Staff**: Nurses, specialists, and other healthcare workers are often not deployed effectively.
- **High Rates of No-Shows**: Missed appointments contribute to lost productivity and wasted resources.

Supply Chain Mismanagement

Supply chain inefficiencies are another source of waste:

- **Overstocking Supplies**: Poor inventory management leads to expired or unused medical supplies.
- **Improper Disposal**: Medical waste is frequently mishandled, adding unnecessary costs.
- **Overuse of Single-Use Items**: Items intended for single use often replace sustainable alternatives unnecessarily.

Financial and Human Costs of Waste

The financial toll of waste is staggering. Studies estimate that roughly 25% of healthcare spending in the U.S. is wasteful, amounting to hundreds of billions of dollars annually. Beyond the monetary impact, these inefficiencies have profound consequences for patients:

- **Delays in Care**: Wasteful practices lead to longer wait times and delayed treatments.

- **Unnecessary Procedures**: Patients undergo procedures that offer little benefit, increasing the risk of complications.

- **Missed Opportunities for Better Health**: Resources spent on wasteful practices could be redirected toward preventative care and better patient outcomes.

The Profit Motive: A Barrier to Change

The profit-driven nature of the healthcare system exacerbates these inefficiencies. Profit-first priorities manifest in several ways:

- **Denial of Necessary Care**: Insurance companies often deny treatments to cut costs.

- **Focus on High-Profit Procedures**: Preventative care and less profitable treatments are deprioritized.

- **Inflated Drug Prices**: Pharmaceutical companies leverage patent protections to charge exorbitant prices.

Toward a Solution: Eliminating Waste

To address these inefficiencies, systemic reforms are necessary:

- **Streamlined Administrative Processes**: Standardized billing systems and electronic health records can reduce overhead costs.

- **Emphasis on Preventative Care**: Investing in preventative measures can reduce the need for costly treatments.
- **Value-Based Payment Models**: Incentivizing providers based on patient outcomes rather than volume of services can encourage more efficient care.
- **Improved Inventory Management**: Optimizing supply chain practices can prevent overstocking and waste.
- **Regulation of Drug Prices**: Allowing government negotiation of drug prices can make medications more affordable.

Conclusion

The waste embedded in the U.S. healthcare system is not an inevitability; it is a consequence of systemic flaws rooted in profit-driven priorities. Eliminating waste requires bold action, from reducing administrative burdens to fostering a culture that prioritizes patient well-being over corporate profits. By addressing these inefficiencies, we can move closer to a healthcare system that serves everyone—efficiently, effectively, and equitably.

Chapter 2

The Cost of Prioritizing Profits Over People

Healthcare is a human right, but in the United States, profit-driven systems have undermined the principles of equitable access, resulting in unnecessary suffering and loss of life. As the wealthiest nation on Earth, the U.S. spends more per capita on healthcare than any other country, yet outcomes often lag behind those of nations with universal systems. This paradox raises an essential question: why do we pay so much for so little?

A Historical Struggle for Care

From the Civil War to the present, the fight for accessible healthcare has faced consistent resistance from entrenched interests prioritizing profit over public welfare. During the Civil War, the Union Army's efforts to set up hospitals and improve surgical methods showed how government intervention could save lives. However, the lack of medical supplies and trained personnel led to more deaths from disease than from battle injuries. Diseases like smallpox, dysentery, and typhoid fever ravaged soldiers, highlighting the need for organized, well-funded healthcare systems.

At the turn of the 20th century, President Theodore Roosevelt recognized the need for public healthcare. Yet, progress was thwarted by opposition from businesses and medical organizations. In steel mills and other dangerous industries, corporations began providing limited healthcare to retain workers. However, these efforts were more about maintaining a workforce than addressing broader public health needs.

The American Association of Labor Legislation (AALL) proposed solutions to support workers and their families, but opposition from the American Medical Association (AMA) and private insurers stalled these efforts. By prioritizing profits, these entities denied countless people the care they needed.

The Modern Cost of Profit-Driven Systems

For-profit healthcare exacerbates inequalities and erodes the quality of care. In 2023, a study revealed that Medicare patients in private equity-owned hospitals faced higher rates of hospital-acquired complications, illustrating how profit motives can jeopardize patient safety. Meanwhile, corporate insurers routinely reject claims for necessary care, forcing patients to pay out of pocket or forgo treatment altogether. This system leaves millions burdened by medical debt, a uniquely American crisis.

Large hospital systems have also contributed to the problem by closing facilities in lower-income communities, effectively abandoning the most vulnerable populations. When hospitals prioritize financial performance over community health, they deepen disparities and force patients to travel long distances for care—if they can afford it.

The Global Comparison

Countries with single-payer systems consistently achieve better outcomes at lower costs. In nations like Canada, the United Kingdom, and Germany, healthcare is treated as a public good, not a commodity. These countries spend significantly less on healthcare as a percentage of GDP, yet their citizens enjoy longer life expectancies, lower infant mortality rates, and higher patient satisfaction.

In contrast, the U.S. healthcare system's inefficiencies are staggering. Administrative costs account for nearly 25% of healthcare expenditures, driven by the complexity of billing and insurance negotiations. These funds could be redirected toward patient care, but the current system prioritizes profit margins over efficiency.

The Cycle of Financial Strain

One of the most insidious effects of the profit-driven model is how it traps individuals in a cycle of financial strain. Many Americans work multiple jobs to pay for basic needs, leaving little time to educate themselves about the benefits of single-payer healthcare. This lack of awareness perpetuates the status quo, as people struggle to advocate for systemic change while merely trying to survive.

Lessons from History: Missed Opportunities

Throughout the 20th century, leaders like Franklin D. Roosevelt, Harry Truman, and Lyndon Johnson made strides toward universal healthcare, but their efforts were often thwarted by powerful lobbies. For example, FDR's initial plans for national healthcare were derailed by the AMA, and Truman's proposals were dismissed amid anti-communist rhetoric.

Even when progress was made, such as with Medicare and Medicaid in 1965, it came at the cost of narrowing the focus to specific populations. Broader plans that could have benefited all Americans were repeatedly shelved, leaving millions to rely on an inefficient and inequitable system.

A Way Forward

The U.S. healthcare system's failures are not inevitable; they are the result of choices. Prioritizing people over profits would mean adopting a single-payer model that ensures access to care for all. Such a system could eliminate administrative waste, reduce costs, and improve outcomes.

The question remains: how many more lives will be lost before we recognize that healthcare is too important to be left to the whims of profit? By learning from history and embracing proven models, we can build a system that serves everyone, not just the privileged few.

Chapter 3

Rebuilding Trust in a Collapsing Healthcare System

Healthcare is a cornerstone of societal well-being, yet trust in the system has been eroding steadily in recent years. A confluence of negative patient experiences, profit-driven motives, lack of transparency, and systemic inequalities have led many to feel alienated and skeptical about the care they receive. This distrust has profound implications for public health, from lower patient engagement to worse outcomes. To restore confidence, it is imperative to address these issues head-on and rebuild the integrity of the healthcare system.

The Roots of Distrust in Healthcare

Negative Patient Experiences

Patients' personal encounters with the healthcare system often define their perception of its reliability. Instances of rushed appointments, dismissive attitudes, misdiagnoses, and poor bedside manner leave patients feeling unheard and undervalued. According to a 2022 survey published in *The Lancet*, 43% of respondents felt their concerns were not adequately addressed by their healthcare providers. Such experiences create a barrier to trust, discouraging individuals from seeking timely care.

Financial Incentives Over Patient Well-Being

The prioritization of profit over patient care is another critical factor undermining trust. The proliferation of for-profit healthcare entities has fostered widespread concern that financial motives may influence treatment decisions. A 2023 *New York Times* investigation revealed that hospitals owned by private equity firms often focus on cost-cutting measures that compromise patient safety, such as reducing staff levels and prioritizing lucrative services over essential ones. Patients who perceive their care as transactional are less likely to trust their providers.

Lack of Transparency

Complex billing practices, opaque insurance policies, and unclear treatment costs exacerbate feelings of distrust. Patients often receive medical bills that are incomprehensible or unexpected, further fueling the perception that the system is designed to exploit rather than help. A 2021 study by *Health Affairs* found that 70% of patients struggled to understand their medical bills, and 56% delayed or avoided care due to cost-related confusion.

Misinformation and Distrust in Institutions

The rise of misinformation online and societal distrust in institutions have also taken a toll. During the COVID-19 pandemic, conflicting messages from public health officials, political leaders, and media outlets deepened skepticism about medical advice. A 2020 survey by the *Pew Research Center* found that only 29% of Americans trusted the government to handle the pandemic effectively. Such widespread doubt erodes faith not only in public health efforts but also in individual healthcare providers.

Disparities in Access and Quality of Care

Unequal access to healthcare based on socioeconomic status, race, and geographic location continues to alienate marginalized populations. For example, a 2022 report by the *Kaiser Family Foundation* highlighted that Black Americans are 40% more likely to die from preventable conditions than white Americans due to disparities in care. When individuals perceive the system as inequitable, trust erodes further.

Poor Communication

Effective communication is at the heart of any trustworthy relationship, yet healthcare providers often fall short. The use of medical jargon, failure to address patient concerns, and insufficient time spent explaining diagnoses or treatment plans leave patients feeling disengaged. This lack of connection undermines the patient-provider relationship and diminishes confidence in care.

Strategies for Rebuilding Trust

To address these pervasive issues, healthcare systems must adopt a comprehensive approach focused on transparency, accountability, and patient-centered care.

Prioritize Patient-Centered Care

Healthcare providers must prioritize listening to patients, addressing their concerns, and involving them in decision-making processes. A patient-centered approach fosters a sense of partnership and respect, which are essential for rebuilding trust. According to a 2023 article in *The Washington Post*, patient satisfaction scores improved by 25% in hospitals that implemented shared decision-making protocols.

Transparency in Costs and Treatment Options

Patients deserve to understand the financial and medical implications of their care. Clear communication about costs, risks, and benefits can alleviate confusion and build confidence. For example, the introduction of online cost estimators by several healthcare systems has been well-received, with a 2021 *JAMA* study showing a 15% reduction in billing disputes.

Improve Provider Training

Healthcare professionals should receive robust training in communication skills, cultural competency, and empathy. Programs like the Cleveland Clinic's "Communicate with H.E.A.R.T." initiative, which trains staff to engage with patients effectively, have demonstrated significant improvements in trust and satisfaction.

Community Engagement

Building trust at the local level is crucial, particularly in underserved communities. Healthcare organizations should actively engage with diverse populations to address concerns, educate about healthcare options, and demonstrate commitment to equity. Initiatives like mobile clinics and community health fairs have proven effective in fostering trust.

Safeguard Data Privacy

Data privacy breaches have heightened fears about the misuse of sensitive medical information. Healthcare organizations must implement stringent data protection measures and communicate transparently about how patient data is used. According to a 2023 *Harvard Business Review* article, institutions that prioritized data security reported a 20% increase in patient trust.

Address Systemic Inequalities

Eliminating disparities in access to care and quality of treatment is essential for restoring trust. Policies aimed at expanding Medicaid, increasing funding for community health centers, and recruiting diverse healthcare providers can help bridge these gaps.

Promote Healthcare Literacy

Educating patients about navigating the healthcare system empowers them to advocate for themselves. Initiatives like the National Action Plan to Improve Health Literacy have shown promise in enhancing patient understanding and engagement.

Accountability and Quality Improvement

Healthcare systems must establish robust mechanisms for monitoring and improving care quality. Holding providers accountable for patient outcomes not only improves care but also reinforces public confidence in the system's integrity.

Conclusion

Rebuilding trust in the healthcare system is both a moral imperative and a practical necessity. By addressing the root causes of distrust and committing to transparency, equity, and patient-centered care, healthcare organizations can restore the confidence of those they serve. Trust is the foundation of effective healthcare, and its restoration will benefit not only individual patients but also the broader health of society.

Chapter 4

A Public System Incentivizes Prevention

One of the most compelling arguments for a public healthcare system is its inherent incentive to prioritize preventative care. Unlike private systems driven by profit, public healthcare systems are designed to maintain the overall health of the population. By focusing on prevention, these systems reduce the financial burden of treating advanced illnesses and improve the quality of life for citizens. This chapter explores the key differences between public and private healthcare systems regarding prevention and outlines actionable solutions to address the disparities.

The Case for Prevention in Public Healthcare

Public healthcare systems are funded through taxes, meaning their financial stability depends on keeping populations healthy and minimizing costly interventions. This creates a natural alignment between public health goals and financial incentives. Preventative care—including screenings, vaccinations, and education—is central to this model. For example, public systems often invest in programs to address the root causes of chronic diseases such as diabetes, heart disease, and cancer by promoting healthy behaviors and early detection.

In the United Kingdom, for instance, the National Health Service (NHS) offers free preventative screenings and wellness checks, which have been shown to reduce the incidence of advanced diseases. Similarly, countries like Sweden and Canada prioritize maternal care and childhood vaccinations, leading to lower infant mortality rates and healthier populations overall. These initiatives highlight how prevention is not only ethically sound but also economically efficient for publicly funded systems.

Challenges in Private Healthcare Systems

In contrast, private healthcare systems operate under a profit-driven model that often prioritizes immediate, billable procedures over long-term health outcomes. The traditional fee-for-service payment structure incentivizes providers to perform more tests and procedures, sometimes leading to over-treatment and unnecessary interventions. While these actions may increase revenue, they do little to address the root causes of illness or promote overall health.

Moreover, private systems may neglect preventative care for populations that cannot afford it, exacerbating health disparities. For example, individuals in the U.S. who lack insurance or have high-deductible plans often delay or forego preventative measures, increasing their risk of severe illness and costly hospitalizations. Studies have shown that countries with privatized healthcare systems, like the U.S., spend more on healthcare per capita yet achieve worse health outcomes compared to nations with public systems.

Value-Based Care: Bridging the Gap

One promising approach to addressing these discrepancies is the adoption of value-based care models. These models shift the focus from the volume of services provided to the quality of outcomes achieved. Under value-based care, healthcare providers are rewarded for keeping patients healthy and preventing illnesses rather than for performing procedures. This incentivizes early intervention, chronic disease management, and patient education—key pillars of preventative care.

For example, the Centers for Medicare & Medicaid Services (CMS) in the U.S. have piloted value-based programs that financially reward hospitals for reducing readmission rates and improving patient outcomes. Preliminary data suggests that these programs can both reduce costs and enhance care quality, demonstrating the potential for preventative-focused incentives within even a predominantly private system.

Key Differences Between Public and Private Systems

Public Healthcare:

- **Population-Based Focus:** Public systems aim to improve health outcomes for the entire population, reducing long-term costs by preventing diseases before they escalate.

- **Emphasis on Prevention:** Governments invest in wellness programs, routine screenings, and public health campaigns to address widespread health concerns.

- **Budget Constraints:** Fixed budgets encourage judicious use of resources, often prioritizing cost-effective preventative measures over expensive treatments.

Private Healthcare:

- **Profit Motive:** Revenue generation often takes precedence, leading to an emphasis on high-cost treatments and procedures.

- **Fee-for-Service Model:** Payment structures reward volume over value, encouraging over-testing and unnecessary interventions.

- **Patient Choice:** While private systems allow for more choice, they may prioritize convenience over comprehensive preventative strategies.

Policy Recommendations to Prioritize Prevention

To create a system that incentivizes prevention across both public and private sectors, several key actions can be taken:

1 Adopt Value-Based Care Models: Transition payment structures to reward providers for achieving positive health outcomes, such as lower rates of chronic disease and hospital readmissions.

2 Implement Performance Metrics: Develop and track specific metrics for preventative care, such as vaccination rates, early detection screenings, and patient education initiatives.

3 Expand Public Health Campaigns: Launch nationwide programs to educate citizens about the benefits of preventative care, healthy lifestyles, and regular check-ups.

4 Enhance Provider Training: Train healthcare professionals in effective communication and prevention strategies to empower patients to take charge of their health.

5 Ensure Accessibility: Remove financial barriers to preventative care by expanding insurance coverage for screenings, vaccinations, and wellness visits.

6 Promote Population Health Management: Encourage healthcare organizations to take responsibility for the health outcomes of their entire patient population, incentivizing early intervention and comprehensive care.

Conclusion

A public healthcare system's focus on prevention not only aligns with ethical principles but also delivers tangible financial and societal benefits. By reducing the prevalence of preventable diseases, such systems improve quality of life and curb healthcare costs. As private systems face growing criticism for prioritizing profits over patient well-being, the need for preventative-focused reforms becomes increasingly urgent. Through value-based care models, improved access, and robust public health initiatives, it is possible to create a system that genuinely prioritizes health over profit, benefiting individuals and society as a whole.

Chapter 5

Best Examples of Public Healthcare Systems Around the World

One of the most pressing questions in healthcare is how to deliver high-quality care to the largest number of people at the most reasonable cost. While every country faces unique challenges, some nations have excelled in creating public healthcare systems that provide exceptional care for the money spent. This chapter examines the best examples of public healthcare systems globally, highlighting key components and practices that make them successful.

What Makes a Public Healthcare System Effective?

A top-performing public healthcare system typically shares the following characteristics:

1 Universal Coverage: Ensures that all citizens have access to healthcare services, regardless of income or employment status.

2 Strong Primary Care: Prioritizes preventative care

and early intervention through accessible primary care providers.

3 Integrated Care Delivery: Facilitates seamless patient care through coordination between healthcare providers and specialties.

4 Quality Assurance and Monitoring: Regularly evaluates healthcare quality using performance metrics and data analysis.

5 Efficient Financing: Combines funding sources, such as taxes, employer contributions, and government subsidies, to ensure financial sustainability.

6 Skilled Healthcare Workforce: Employs sufficient numbers of qualified medical professionals across all specialties.

7 Public Health Initiatives: Invests in programs to prevent diseases and promote population health.

8 Technology Adoption: Leverages digital tools for improved patient care and administrative efficiency.

9 Equity and Access: Reduces disparities in healthcare access caused by socioeconomic factors.

10 Strong Governance: Implements clear policies and oversight mechanisms to manage the system effectively.

Countries with the Best Public Healthcare Systems

Norway

- **System Type:** Tax-funded universal healthcare system.

- **Strengths:** Norway is known for its high-quality care and accessibility. The system's emphasis on preventative care and robust primary care services helps minimize the need for costly interventions. Patients have access to a wide range of services, from general practitioners to specialized treatments, without facing significant financial barriers.

- **Challenges:** Long wait times for certain procedures remain an issue.

Australia

- **System Type:** Medicare, a universal system combining public funding and private options.

- **Strengths:** Since its inception in 1986, Australia's Medicare system has provided free or low-cost access to public hospital services and general practitioners. Preventative care, such as cancer screenings and immunizations, is a major focus.

- **Challenges:** Rural and remote areas sometimes face shortages of medical professionals.

Germany

- **System Type:** Social health insurance model.

- **Strengths:** Germany's "sickness funds" mandate universal coverage, ensuring comprehensive care for all. The system emphasizes preventative care, strong patient-provider communication, and accessibility to both public and private hospitals.

- **Challenges:** High administrative costs and growing demands on the system due to an aging population.

France

- **System Type:** Tax-based public healthcare with optional private insurance.

- **Strengths:** France consistently ranks high for patient satisfaction due to its excellent provider-patient ratio and comprehensive services. Public healthcare is considered on par with private options, and patients can choose their providers without network restrictions.

- **Challenges:** Rising healthcare costs threaten the long-term sustainability of the system.

Japan

- **System Type:** Publicly funded, with mandatory insurance for all residents.

- **Strengths:** Japan excels in preventative care, with routine health screenings and early detection programs contributing to some of the highest life expectancies globally. The system is highly efficient and cost-effective.

- **Challenges:** Hospitals and clinics face funding shortages due to Japan's aging population.

United Kingdom

• **System Type:** National Health Service (NHS), a tax-funded single-payer system.

• **Strengths:** The NHS prioritizes primary care, offering comprehensive and free-at-point-of-service healthcare. It is lauded for its equity and accessibility.

• **Challenges:** Funding shortfalls and workforce pressures have led to longer wait times in recent years.

Switzerland

• **System Type:** Mandatory health insurance with competitive private insurers.

• **Strengths:** Swiss residents are required to have health insurance, which guarantees access to high-quality care. The system's competition between insurers keeps costs relatively contained while maintaining high standards.

• **Challenges:** Out-of-pocket costs can still be a burden for low-income families.

Canada

• **System Type:** Single-payer healthcare system.

• **Strengths:** Canada provides universal healthcare funded by taxes, focusing on equitable access. Its emphasis on primary care helps manage chronic diseases effectively.

• **Challenges:** Like other systems, Canada faces challenges with wait times for specialized procedures.

Lessons from Top-Performing Countries

Universal Coverage

Countries like Norway and Japan demonstrate that universal healthcare systems can provide high-quality care when financed sustainably. By ensuring access for all citizens, these systems reduce disparities in health outcomes.

Preventative Care

The emphasis on prevention in Japan and Australia—through routine screenings and wellness programs—keeps populations healthier and reduces long-term costs.

Efficient Administration

Germany and Switzerland's structured financing models minimize wasteful spending while ensuring resources are allocated effectively.

Equity and Accessibility

The UK's NHS and Canada's single-payer system excel at prioritizing equitable access, ensuring that socioeconomic status does not determine the quality of care received.

Conclusion

The best public healthcare systems around the world share common goals: improving population health, reducing costs, and ensuring equitable access. While each system operates within unique cultural and economic contexts, their successes provide valuable lessons for designing effective healthcare models. By adopting and adapting these strategies, countries can move closer to achieving the ideal of healthcare for all.

Chapter 6

Setting Goals and Priorities for Transitioning to a Public Healthcare System

Introduction

The transition from a profit-based healthcare system to a public healthcare model in the United States requires a phased approach, carefully balancing immediate needs with long-term goals. By focusing initially on prevention, addressing systemic issues like opioid overuse, and creating robust care mechanisms for vulnerable populations such as the homeless, we can lay the groundwork for a healthcare system that prioritizes health over profit.

This chapter outlines a five-year and ten-year plan for achieving these objectives, along with proposed budgets and actionable steps to guide the transition.

The Five-Year Plan: Building the Foundation

Goals

1 Prioritize Preventative Care:

○ Expand access to screenings, immunizations, and health education programs.

○ Establish community health centers in underserved areas.

2 Address Opioid Overuse:

○ Implement nationwide prescription monitoring programs.

○ Expand access to addiction treatment and recovery services.

3 Care for the Homeless:

○ Develop integrated health and housing initiatives.

○ Ensure access to mental health and substance abuse services.

4 Prepare for Transition:

○ Streamline administrative processes.

○ Pilot public healthcare models in select states.

Action Steps

1 Expand Preventative Services:

○ Allocate S15 billion annually to increase funding for public health campaigns focused on chronic disease prevention, healthy lifestyles, and vaccination outreach.

○ Incentivize primary care providers to offer annual wellness visits, nutrition counseling, and screenings.

2 Combat the Opioid Crisis:

○ Invest $10 billion annually in treatment programs, including medication-assisted treatments (MATs) such as methadone and buprenorphine.

○ Launch public awareness campaigns to destigmatize addiction and promote recovery resources.

○ Regulate pharmaceutical companies and enforce stricter guidelines for opioid prescriptions.

3 Homeless Healthcare and Housing:

○ Allocate $12 billion annually to fund healthcare programs tailored to homeless populations.

○ Expand "housing first" initiatives that provide permanent housing combined with wraparound healthcare services.

4 Pilot Public Healthcare Models:

○ Invest $5 billion annually in states like California and Vermont to test single-payer systems, collecting data to inform national implementation.

○ Streamline electronic health records (EHRs) to reduce administrative costs.

Budget Overview (Annual):

• Preventative care: $15 billion

- Opioid crisis response: $10 billion
- Homeless healthcare: $12 billion
- Pilot programs and administration: $5 billion
- **Total:** $42 billion

The Ten-Year Plan: Scaling and Integration

Goals

1 Universal Coverage:

○ Extend public healthcare to all citizens through a single-payer system.

2 Reduce Healthcare Disparities:

○ Address systemic inequities affecting marginalized communities.

3 Strengthen Preventative Care:

○ Fully integrate preventative care into all aspects of the healthcare system.

4 Sustain and Expand Opioid Recovery Programs:

○ Transition opioid response programs into long-term support networks.

5 Permanent Solutions for Homeless Healthcare:

○ Ensure universal healthcare includes targeted programs for homeless populations.

Action Steps

1 Implement Universal Coverage:

○ Roll out Medicare for All with a gradual expansion starting with children, low-income families, and seniors.

○ Simplify insurance processes by phasing out private insurance for basic care and transitioning to government-funded models.

2 Address Disparities:

○ Allocate $20 billion annually to initiatives that focus on rural health, minority health, and gender equity in healthcare access.

○ Increase funding for community health workers to bridge gaps in care.

3 Strengthen Preventative Measures:

○ Incorporate preventative care metrics into healthcare provider evaluations.

○ Introduce workplace wellness programs funded by the government.

4 Sustain Opioid Programs:

○ Expand funding for long-term care facilities, community recovery programs, and mental health integration.

○ Penalize non-compliance by pharmaceutical companies with strict drug control regulations.

5 Healthcare for Homeless Populations:

○ Establish permanent clinics within shelters and low-income housing developments.

○ Collaborate with cities to fund mobile clinics offering basic healthcare and mental health services.

Budget Overview (Annual):

- Universal coverage expansion: $150 billion
- Disparities reduction: $20 billion
- Strengthening prevention: $25 billion
- Sustained opioid recovery programs: $15 billion
- Permanent homeless care solutions: $10 billion
- **Total:** $220 billion

Opioid Overuse: A Case Study for Reform

The opioic crisis highlights the need for systemic change. Over 100,000 overdose deaths annually reflect the failure of profit-driven healthcare. A public healthcare system can address this by:

- Regulating pharmaceutical marketing and prescribing practices.
- Funding community-based recovery programs that focus on holistic care.
- Providing free access to life-saving treatments like naloxone.

Impact:

- Reduced overdose deaths by 30% within five years.
- Long-term decrease in addiction rates through prevention and education.

Homeless Healthcare: A Moral and Economic Imperative

Homeless individuals experience disproportionate rates of chronic illness, mental health issues, and substance abuse. Investing in healthcare for this population is both humane and cost-effective.

Key Steps:

1 Integrate Housing and Healthcare:

○ Expand programs like "Housing First," proven to reduce healthcare costs by 40% for participants.

2 Increase Access to Mental Health Services:

○ Co-locate mental health clinics with shelters to ensure accessibility.

3 Mobile Clinics:

○ Deploy mobile units to provide regular check-ups, wound care, and chronic disease management.

Impact:

- Reduction in emergency room visits by 50%.

- Improved life expectancy and quality of life for homeless individuals.

Measuring Success

To ensure accountability, the following metrics should be tracked:

1 Health Outcomes:

○ Reduction in chronic disease prevalence.

○ Increase in life expectancy.

2 Economic Impact:

○ Decrease in healthcare costs as a percentage of GDP.

○ Reduction in uninsured rates.

3 Social Benefits:

○ Improved public perception of healthcare.

○ Increased patient satisfaction.

Conclusion

Transitioning to a public healthcare system in the United States is an ambitious but necessary undertaking. By setting clear goals, focusing on prevention, addressing systemic issues like opioid overuse, and prioritizing vulnerable populations, we can create a healthcare system that is equitable, efficient, and centered on the well-being of all citizens. The five-year and ten-year plans outlined here provide a roadmap to achieving these goals while ensuring fiscal sustainability and measurable improvements in health outcomes.

Chapter 7

Reducing and Neutralizing Opposition to Healthcare for All

The transition to a public healthcare system in the United States faces significant opposition from industries and groups that profit from the current profit-driven system, such as health insurance companies, pharmaceutical corporations, and certain healthcare providers. This chapter explores strategies to address and neutralize resistance to universal healthcare by aligning incentives, building coalitions, and implementing a phased approach over five and ten years.

Understanding the Opposition

The primary opposition to healthcare for all arises from:

1 **Health Insurance Industry**: Profits are driven by premiums, administrative fees, and denial of costly care.

2 Pharmaceutical Companies: High drug prices generate significant revenue.

3 Private Hospitals and Providers: Concerns about reimbursement rates under a public system.

4 Politicians and Lobbyists: Heavily influenced by campaign contributions from the healthcare industry.

5 Public Misconceptions: Fear of increased taxes, rationing, or loss of quality in care.

Neutralizing this opposition requires strategic engagement and policy design that addresses these concerns while building public and political support.

Methods to Reduce Opposition

1 Incentivizing the Insurance Industry:

○ Transition insurers to roles as administrators for a public system.

○ Provide financial incentives for insurers to manage supplemental insurance or administrative services.

○ Offer grants to help companies pivot to other lines of business.

2 Engaging Pharmaceutical Companies:

○ Establish transparent pricing negotiations with guaranteed volume purchasing agreements to protect profits while lowering costs.

○ Invest in public-private partnerships for research and development.

○ Offer incentives for innovation in preventative care and affordable treatments.

3 Addressing Private Providers:

○ Ensure fair and transparent reimbursement rates that reflect quality outcomes.

○ Create pilot programs to demonstrate how universal healthcare reduces administrative burdens and improves care delivery.

○ Introduce value-based payment models that reward better patient outcomes.

4 Engaging Policymakers and Lobbyists:

○ Focus on bipartisan framing of healthcare as a moral and economic imperative.

○ Highlight cost savings and benefits for businesses that no longer need to provide employer-sponsored insurance.

○ Build public pressure through grassroots advocacy.

5 Educating the Public:

○ Launch educational campaigns about the benefits of healthcare for all.

○ Address fears with data on cost savings and improved outcomes in other countries.

○ Leverage trusted voices, such as healthcare professionals, to build credibility.

Five-Year Plan

Goal: Lay the groundwork for transitioning to a public healthcare system by building stakeholder buy-in, implementing pilot programs, and establishing key legislative frameworks.

1 Year 1: Engage Stakeholders

○ Create a national task force comprising representatives from insurance companies, pharmaceutical firms, hospitals, and patient advocacy groups.

○ Host public forums to gather input and address concerns.

○ Introduce legislation to establish value-based care pilot programs.

2 Year 2: Educate the Public

○ Launch a national media campaign highlighting the benefits of universal healthcare, including reduced costs and improved access.

○ Partner with community organizations to provide localized education.

3 Year 3: Pilot Programs

○ Test regional public healthcare models in diverse settings, such as urban and rural areas.

○ Demonstrate cost savings and improved outcomes through pilot programs.

4 Year 4: Incentivize Transition

○ Offer tax credits or grants to health insurers transitioning to administrative roles.

○ Introduce legislation requiring transparent pricing for drugs and procedures.

5 Year 5: Build Political Momentum

○ Publish findings from pilot programs to showcase success.

○ Build bipartisan coalitions in Congress to support broader healthcare reform legislation.

Ten-Year Plan

Goal: Fully implement a public healthcare system while ensuring financial sustainability and stakeholder alignment.

1 Years 6-7: Phase One Implementation

○ Pass comprehensive healthcare reform legislation, establishing universal coverage funded through taxes and employer contributions.

○ Begin national rollout of public insurance options, with private insurers offering supplemental plans.

○ Expand negotiation frameworks for pharmaceuticals to achieve equitable pricing.

2 Years 8-9: Address System Gaps

○ Use data from the initial rollout to address disparities in access and care quality.

○ Invest in healthcare infrastructure, such as clinics in underserved areas.

○ Implement programs for workforce training to address provider shortages.

3 Year 10: Full Implementation and Evaluation

○ Ensure universal enrollment in the public system.

○ Continuously evaluate system performance and make adjustments to address inefficiencies.

○ Build international partnerships to share best practices and maintain global competitiveness.

Conclusion

Neutralizing opposition to healthcare for all requires thoughtful, phased strategies that align financial incentives, demonstrate tangible benefits, and build public trust. By engaging stakeholders, incentivizing industries, and addressing public concerns, the United

States can create a sustainable, equitable healthcare system that prioritizes the well-being of all citizens. This transition will take time and effort, but the long-term benefits far outweigh the costs, paving the way for a healthier and more just society.

Chapter 8

Preventing Hospitalization Through Government Action

To achieve universal healthcare that prioritizes prevention, the government must actively address the root causes of hospitalizations. Many of these causes stem from systemic issues, such as unhealthy diets, chemical exposure, addiction, and environmental hazards. By tackling these issues head-on, the government can reduce hospital admissions, improve population health, and lower healthcare costs.

Reducing the Consumption of Highly Processed Foods

Highly processed foods have been linked to chronic diseases like obesity, diabetes, and cancer. Governments can take action to curb their consumption through regulation, taxation, education, and incentives.

1 Regulations on Processed Food Production

○ **Ban Harmful Ingredients:** Prohibit the use of additives, artificial trans fats, and preservatives linked to health risks.

○ **Labeling Requirements:** Mandate clear and prominent labeling on all processed foods, highlighting unhealthy ingredients like added sugars, sodium, and unhealthy fats.

2 Taxation Policies

○ **Sugary Drinks and Junk Food Taxes:** Introduce taxes on sugary beverages and ultra-processed snacks, redirecting revenue to fund public health programs.

○ **Subsidize Healthy Foods:** Reduce the cost of fruits, vegetables, and whole foods by providing subsidies to farmers and retailers.

3 Public Education Campaigns

○ Launch nationwide campaigns to educate the public about the dangers of processed foods and the benefits of a whole-food diet.

○ Partner with schools to teach children about nutrition and cooking healthy meals from an early age.

4 Incentives for Food Industry Reform

○ Offer tax credits to food manufacturers that reformulate products to meet health standards.

○ Provide grants for research into healthier food alternatives and sustainable agriculture practices.

• • •

Addressing Opioid Addiction in Hospitals

The opioid crisis is a major driver of hospitalizations and long-term health issues. The government must adopt a multi-faceted approach to prevent addiction and provide better pain management alternatives.

1 Stricter Prescription Guidelines

○ Enforce limits on opioid prescriptions, ensuring they are only used when absolutely necessary.

○ Promote the use of non-opioid pain management techniques, such as physical therapy, acupuncture, and mindfulness practices.

2 Mandatory Provider Training

○ Require healthcare providers to undergo training on responsible opioid prescribing and addiction prevention.

○ Introduce continuing education programs on the latest non-addictive pain treatments.

3 Expand Access to Addiction Treatment

○ Increase funding for medication-assisted treatment (MAT) programs, such as those using methadone or buprenorphine.

○ Establish addiction treatment centers in underserved areas and integrate these services into primary care settings.

4 Accountability Measures for Hospitals

○ Tie hospital funding and performance metrics to responsible opioid prescribing practices.

○ Implement systems to track and monitor opioid prescriptions and patient outcomes.

Caring for the Homeless to Prevent Hospitalizations

Homelessness is a significant driver of hospitalizations due to untreated chronic illnesses, exposure to harsh conditions, and lack of preventive care. Addressing homelessness is essential to improving public health.

1 Housing First Programs

○ Provide permanent, affordable housing to homeless individuals without requiring prior treatment or sobriety.

○ Pair housing with access to healthcare, mental health services, and job training programs.

2 Mobile Health Clinics

○ Deploy mobile clinics to provide preventive care, vaccinations, and screenings to homeless populations.

○ Integrate mobile clinics with local shelters and outreach programs.

3 Expand Medicaid Coverage

○ Ensure Medicaid covers comprehensive care for homeless individuals, including mental health and substance abuse treatment.

○ Streamline enrollment processes to reduce barriers to access.

4 Employment and Social Services Support

○ Create programs that connect homeless individuals with stable employment opportunities.

○ Increase funding for social workers to assist in navigating housing, healthcare, and employment systems.

Reducing Exposure to Harmful Chemicals and Plastics in the Food Supply

The contamination of food by harmful chemicals and plastics contributes to a variety of health issues, including cancer, hormonal disorders, and developmental problems. The government can play a pivotal role in minimizing these risks.

1 Regulations on Chemical Usage

○ Ban or strictly regulate the use of harmful chemicals, such as BPA, phthalates, and PFAS, in food packaging and production.

○ Require comprehensive safety testing of all chemicals before they are approved for use in the food industry.

2 Monitoring and Enforcement

○ Strengthen the Food and Drug Administration (FDA) and Environmental Protection Agency (EPA) to monitor and enforce safety standards.

○ Conduct regular inspections of food production facilities to ensure compliance with safety regulations.

3 Incentives for Safer Alternatives

○ Provide grants to companies developing biodegradable, non-toxic food packaging alternatives.

○ Offer tax breaks to manufacturers that adopt safer, environmentally friendly production practices.

4 Public Awareness and Education

○ Launch campaigns to educate consumers about the risks of chemicals in food and how to avoid them.

○ Encourage the use of reusable and safe food storage options, such as glass or stainless steel.

Incentivizing Healthy Lifestyles

Encouraging individuals to adopt healthier lifestyles can significantly reduce hospital admissions and improve overall public health. The government can implement various measures to promote wellness and prevention.

1 Financial Incentives for Healthy Behavior

○ Provide tax deductions or rebates for individuals who participate in wellness programs, gym memberships, or regular health screenings.

○ Offer discounts on health insurance premiums for maintaining a healthy BMI, quitting smoking, or attending preventive care appointments.

2 Community Health Initiatives

○ Fund the creation of public parks, recreational facilities, and safe walking or biking paths.

○ Support local farmers' markets and community gardens to increase access to fresh, healthy food.

3 Workplace Wellness Programs

○ Mandate employers to provide wellness programs, such as stress management workshops, fitness classes, and healthy food options.

○ Offer grants to small businesses to implement workplace health initiatives.

4 School-Based Interventions

○ Introduce mandatory physical education classes and nutritious school meal programs.

○ Educate students on healthy habits through comprehensive health curricula.

A Holistic Approach to Prevention

By addressing the root causes of poor health—from diet and addiction to environmental hazards and homelessness—the government can significantly reduce the burden on hospitals and improve population health. These actions require collaboration across sectors, robust funding, and a commitment to prioritizing prevention over profit.

Through bold policies and sustained investment, the vision of a healthier, more equitable healthcare system can become a reality. It begins with reducing the conditions that lead to hospitalizations and fostering a culture of health and wellness for all.

Chapter 9

The Supporters of Healthcare for All

A universal healthcare system has the potential to unify diverse groups who may otherwise seem at odds with each other. The movement for healthcare for all is not only about ensuring access to medical care; it's about improving the quality of life, reducing financial strain, and promoting a healthier, more productive society. As such, different groups—driven by varied motivations—have a stake in seeing healthcare become a right rather than a privilege. This chapter explores these groups, their motivations, and the impact of such a shift on individuals and businesses alike.

1. Progressive Democrats and Social Justice Advocates

At the forefront of the healthcare for all movement are progressive Democrats, social justice advocates, and those fighting for economic equality. For these groups, universal healthcare represents a moral imperative. They argue that healthcare is a fundamental human right and that no one should suffer or die due to their inability to pay for medical care. Their motivations are centered around the belief in reducing inequalities in access to healthcare and achieving a fairer society.

These groups also recognize that universal healthcare would eliminate disparities based on race, income, and geography. For example, low-income families and marginalized communities would have access to the same quality of care as wealthier individuals, helping to address long-standing health disparities.

2. Healthcare Workers and Providers

Healthcare workers, including doctors, nurses, and other healthcare professionals, are another key constituency that could support healthcare for all. Although they may initially be concerned about changes to reimbursement models, the long-term benefits are clear: reducing administrative burdens, eliminating the need for complicated insurance negotiations, and focusing on patient care rather than navigating insurance systems.

Additionally, healthcare workers often express frustration with the inequities in the current system—where many people delay or avoid necessary care due to high costs. With universal healthcare, they would be able to focus on providing care to their patients without having to consider whether or not patients can afford the treatment.

3. Business Leaders and Economists

Another unexpected group of potential supporters includes many business leaders and economists. While some might initially oppose the idea of universal healthcare due to concerns about taxes and government spending, others recognize the long-term economic benefits that could result from such a system. Healthcare costs are a significant burden on businesses, particularly small businesses, which often struggle to provide health insurance to their employees. By shifting the burden of healthcare to the government, companies would be able to reduce overhead costs and focus on growing their businesses.

Moreover, a healthier workforce would lead to higher productivity, lower absenteeism, and reduced turnover—all of which are beneficial to businesses in the long run. Furthermore, with a more equitable system, businesses could be freed from the responsibility of providing healthcare benefits, making the employment landscape more competitive.

4. Trump's Make America Great Again (MAGA) Supporters

It may seem surprising that supporters of former President Donald Trump's "Make America Great Again" movement could align with the healthcare for all initiative. However, there are several compelling reasons why this group could be persuaded to support universal healthcare. First, many MAGA supporters express concern over the rising costs of healthcare, particularly for the working class and middle-income families. The current system places a heavy financial burden on individuals, often leaving them vulnerable to medical debt and bankruptcy.

A universal healthcare system could resonate with MAGA supporters because it promises to provide affordable and accessible care to all Americans, which directly addresses their concerns about economic inequality. Additionally, MAGA supporters often emphasize nationalism and a desire for the U.S. to be a self-sufficient and strong country. Providing healthcare for all would contribute to a healthier, more productive population, which aligns with these values.

5. Libertarians and Fiscal Conservatives

While libertarians may traditionally oppose government intervention in the economy, there is room for dialogue on universal healthcare. Some libertarians argue that the current healthcare system, which relies on private insurance, is fundamentally flawed and inefficient. They may support a single-payer system as a way to eliminate bureaucratic waste, reduce the need for government subsidies to private insurance companies, and ensure that healthcare is not a commodity dictated by profit motives.

Fiscal conservatives, on the other hand, may see healthcare for all as a way to reduce overall costs in the system. By streamlining administrative processes and eliminating waste, they argue, a universal healthcare system could ultimately save the country money in the long run. The key to convincing fiscal conservatives would be emphasizing the cost-effectiveness of the system, which could potentially lower the financial burden on taxpayers and reduce the national debt.

Benefits for Supporters and Opponents

For Supporters:

1 Reduced Financial Burden: Universal healthcare would alleviate the financial strain of medical bills, which can be catastrophic for individuals and families. People would no longer have to worry about out-of-pocket expenses or being underinsured.

2 Improved Public Health: A healthier population benefits everyone, whether you are receiving care or not. Universal healthcare ensures that diseases are diagnosed and treated early, which reduces the spread of illness and the overall burden on the healthcare system.

3 Greater Economic Stability: With healthcare covered, individuals would have more disposable income to spend in other areas of the economy potentially boosting consumer spending and overall economic growth.

For Opponents:

1 Concerns About Taxes: The primary concern for many opponents of universal healthcare is the potential increase in taxes. However, many proponents argue that the tax increase would be outweighed by the reduction in individual healthcare costs and the broader economic benefits.

2 Government Control and Bureaucracy: Some critics of universal healthcare fear that it would lead to inefficient government control over medical decisions. However, proponents argue that a well-designed system can maintain a balance between government oversight and the autonomy of healthcare providers.

3 Loss of Private Insurance: Some individuals and businesses may worry about the loss of private insurance options and the lack of choice in providers. However, this could be mitigated by offering supplemental insurance for those who prefer additional coverage or specialized care.

Impact on Liability Laws and Workmen's Compensation

With the implementation of universal healthcare, the question of how liability laws and worker's compensation would be affected is crucial. In a single-payer system, most healthcare expenses would be covered by the government. However, employers would still need to provide a safe working environment, and workers would retain the right to compensation if they are injured on the job.

Workmen's compensation laws might need to be modified to reflect the shift in healthcare coverage. Employers would no longer be responsible for covering the healthcare costs of injured workers, but they would still need to cover lost wages and rehabilitation costs. This could lead to a more streamlined process, as the focus would shift from managing healthcare costs to managing workplace safety and recovery.

Negotiation with Insurance Companies

In a healthcare for all system, the need for individuals to negotiate payments with insurance companies would be largely eliminated. The government, as the primary insurer, would set prices for services and medications, creating a standardized system. This would reduce the complexity and frustration of dealing with multiple insurance companies and different policies.

However, some form of negotiation might still exist for those who wish to purchase supplementary private insurance for additional coverage or specialized care. These negotiations would likely focus on supplemental care rather than essential health services, which would be guaranteed by the universal system.

Conclusion

The movement for healthcare for all is not just a matter of ethics or social justice; it has economic, health, and personal implications for a wide range of individuals and groups. From business leaders to healthcare professionals, to the working class and even MAGA supporters, the benefits of universal healthcare are broad and compelling. The transition would likely come with challenges, but the overall outcomes could lead to a more equitable, efficient, and healthier society for all.

Chapter 10

Uniting Forces for Healthcare for All

The journey to making healthcare for all a reality requires the coordinated effort of multiple forces within society: business, government, nonprofit organizations, and everyday citizens. These entities may have different priorities and concerns, but they share a common goal: ensuring that every person, regardless of income, background, or employment status, has access to affordable and comprehensive healthcare. The following chapter will explain how these forces can come together to pass legislation and implement policies that will pave the way for a universal healthcare system.

1. The Vision: Healthcare as a Right, Not a Privilege

The first step in uniting the forces for healthcare for all is creating a shared vision. This vision involves viewing healthcare not as a commodity to be bought and sold based on wealth, but as a basic human right to which every citizen is entitled. The vision must be clear, concise, and inclusive of the various stakeholders who will play a role in this transition.

Business leaders may see the economic benefits of a healthier workforce; government officials may recognize the cost savings of reducing emergency care expenses; nonprofit groups may focus on fairness and equity. Each group must understand how healthcare for all fits into their overarching goals. Through education, dialogue, and collaboration, they will form a united front to push for comprehensive policy reform.

2. The Role of Government: The Legislative Backbone

The government is the central force in enacting healthcare for all through legislation. While public support is essential, the legislative process must be managed carefully to avoid gridlock and opposition. Key government players, including lawmakers, public health officials, and regulatory agencies, will need to be engaged early and often in this process.

Goals:

- **Pass a National Healthcare Act**: This act will outline the fundamental framework for a universal healthcare system, including coverage for every citizen and necessary funding mechanisms.

- **Create a Funding Mechanism**: Sustainable funding must be secured through a mix of taxes, cost savings from the healthcare system's efficiency, and private contributions where appropriate.

- **Streamline Healthcare Administration**: The government must create an efficient system to manage claims, reduce bureaucracy, and establish uniform standards across the country.

Methods:

- **Build a Broad Coalition of Support**: Engage both progressive and conservative lawmakers, business leaders, healthcare providers, and the public to garner broad bipartisan support.

- **Conduct Public Hearings**: Hold forums and hearings to discuss the specific needs of different regions and demographics. This will increase transparency and ensure that all voices are heard.

- **Pilot Programs and Incremental Changes**: Rather than pushing for an immediate, all-encompassing overhaul, start with pilot programs in various states or sectors. Use these as testing grounds to refine the system before scaling up nationwide.

Benchmarks:

- **Year 1-2**: Introduction of legislative proposals and gathering of public feedback. Launch pilot programs in select states or industries.

- **Year 3-4**: Full rollout of national healthcare legislation with a focus on universal coverage for children and low-income individuals. Expansion of existing government-funded programs like Medicaid and Medicare.

- **Year 5**: Introduction of measures for cost control and healthcare efficiency, such as negotiated pricing for pharmaceuticals and streamlined administration.

3. The Business Community: Aligning Economic Interests with Universal Healthcare

Though many businesses, particularly large corporations, are initially wary of the financial implications of universal healthcare, there are significant incentives that could make healthcare for all an attractive proposition. The current employer-based system of healthcare is expensive and burdensome for businesses of all sizes. By shifting the responsibility of providing healthcare to the government, businesses could reduce overhead costs and invest more in innovation and workforce development.

Goals:

- **Reduce Healthcare Costs for Employers**: Businesses want to reduce their healthcare expenditure, which can account for a significant portion of overhead, especially in small and medium-sized businesses.

- **Increase Productivity and Worker Retention**: A healthy workforce is a more productive workforce. Universal healthcare can help lower absenteeism and improve morale.

- **Free Up Resources for Other Benefits**: With the financial burden of healthcare lifted, businesses can focus on offering other employee benefits, such as better wages, educational opportunities, or retirement plans.

Methods:

- **Highlight the Long-Term Economic Benefits**: Create reports and analyses showing the positive effects of universal healthcare on businesses, such as increased productivity, lower turnover rates, and reduced insurance-related expenses.

- **Engage Business Associations**: Work with business leaders and associations like the Chamber of Commerce to spread the message of how universal healthcare will benefit the economy and the private sector.

- **Offer Gradual Transition Plans**: Businesses should be allowed to phase into the new system, giving them time to adjust to the changes and reduce initial resistance.

Benchmarks:

- **Year 1-2**: Establish communication channels between business leaders and policymakers. Begin discussions on how the business community will be integrated into the new healthcare system.

- **Year 3-4**: Roll out pilot programs in certain industries or regions, showing how universal healthcare can work without disrupting business operations.

- **Year 5**: Comprehensive adoption of universal

healthcare, with businesses fully transitioned to the government system.

4. Nonprofits and Advocacy Groups: Driving Public Support

Nonprofit organizations, including healthcare advocacy groups, social justice organizations, and public health advocates, play a critical role in advancing the cause of healthcare for all. These groups provide the grassroots support and public pressure necessary to push lawmakers into action. They also help to educate the public about the benefits of universal healthcare, dispel myths, and address concerns.

Goals:

- **Raise Awareness**: Educate the public about the importance of healthcare as a human right and the economic and health benefits of universal healthcare.

- **Mobilize Voters**: Help to build a powerful voter base that supports healthcare for all through grassroots campaigns and public demonstrations.

- **Secure Funding**: Raise funds to support advocacy efforts, including public awareness campaigns and lobbying activities.

Methods:

- **Public Awareness Campaigns**: Use media, social media, and community outreach to engage the public and shift perceptions about universal healthcare.

• **Lobbying and Political Pressure**: Lobby elected officials to prioritize healthcare reform. Build alliances with progressive lawmakers who are already sympathetic to the cause.

• **Community Engagement**: Organize rallies, town halls, and events that bring together a broad spectrum of people to speak out in favor of universal healthcare.

Benchmarks:

• **Year 1-2**: Launch a nationwide awareness campaign. Mobilize volunteers and activists to educate communities about the benefits of healthcare for all.

• **Year 3-4**: Expand lobbying efforts to ensure that legislators take up the cause of universal healthcare. Start pushing for pilot programs to test the feasibility of universal coverage.

• **Year 5**: Coordinate efforts to ensure the successful passage of national healthcare legislation and work toward full implementation.

5. Inspiring Opponents: Building Consensus Across Divides

While many groups will support healthcare for all, there will be those who oppose it, whether due to ideological beliefs or concerns about the impact on their livelihoods. Winning over these opponents is essential to building the broadest coalition possible.

Methods:

- **Emphasize Cost Savings**: Address concerns about the potential cost of universal healthcare by highlighting how such a system can reduce overall healthcare spending, including costs associated with emergency care and preventable illnesses.

- **Focus on Economic Security**: For small businesses and individuals who fear increased taxes, show how universal healthcare can free up resources for other economic initiatives, such as job creation, innovation, and long-term savings.

- **Promote Freedom of Choice**: Reassure those worried about government control over healthcare that the system will still allow for some level of choice, including options for supplemental private insurance.

Benchmarks:

- **Year 1-2**: Focus on open dialogue with opponents to understand their concerns and provide clear information about the benefits of the new system.

- **Year 3-4**: Introduce compromises and pilot programs that incorporate the concerns of opponents while still working toward the overall goal of universal healthcare.

- **Year 5**: Achieve consensus on the core principles of the healthcare system and successfully transition the nation to a universal coverage model.

6. Two Five-Year Plans: Gradual Implementation

To implement healthcare for all, a two-phase, ten-year plan can guide the process. These plans would allow for incremental changes, with each phase building on the success of the previous one.

First Five-Year Plan (Years 1-5):

- **Phase 1**: Establish pilot programs, expand Medicaid and Medicare, and develop the legislative framework.

- **Phase 2**: Rollout universal coverage for vulnerable populations (low-income, children, the elderly) while addressing business and employer concerns.

- **Phase 3**: Expand coverage to the general population and begin tackling inefficiencies in the current healthcare system.

Second Five-Year Plan (Years 6-10):

- **Phase 1**: Fully integrate all citizens into the healthcare system. Implement national price controls for pharmaceuticals and medical services.

- **Phase 2**: Continue to refine the system based on feedback from businesses, healthcare providers, and citizens. Monitor efficiency and adjust taxes and funding mechanisms as needed.

- **Phase 3**: Evaluate the success of the system and make necessary adjustments to ensure long-term sustainability.

Conclusion

The push for healthcare for all will require cooperation across all sectors of society—government, business, nonprofits, and the general public. Through strategic planning, inclusive dialogue, and careful implementation, healthcare for all can become a reality. By focusing on gradual changes, building a broad coalition, and addressing the concerns of all parties, the movement will gain momentum, eventually leading to a sustainable and equitable healthcare system for every American.

About the Author

Like most Americans, Dan Paul has struggled to get healthcare. Doing it yourself doesn't work well for broken bones and cuts that don't stop bleeding. Born and raised near Lake Wobegon, he played sports, went fishing, and built houses before exploring progressive, radical, and sustainable projects around the US. He wrote this book to make healthcare for everyone.

Also by Dan Paul

Philosophy of Action Design and Multiplicity by Dan Paul

Book 1 Auto Free Design

Book 2 Workers Health Handbook

Book 3 Save Your Life Prevent Hospital Use

Book 4 Coop Owners Handbook

Book 5 Eye on AI Meeting Needs Sustainably

Book 6 Travels on the Nomadic Terrain

Book 7 Tales of the Urban Shaman

Book 8 Housing in the Danger Zone

Book 9 Corona Time

Book 10 Philosophy of Design, Action and Multiplicity

Landlords Against Eviction

Auto Free USA

Websites

https://viaradmedia.org

https://autofreedesign.com

http://workershealthhandbook.com

http://sylphu.com

Social Media

https://www.facebook.com/profile.php?id=61555599616489

https://twitter.com/jonblu

https://www.instagram.com/jonblu61/

Made in the USA
Monee, IL
09 November 2026

67380378R10048